LIVING LIFE
with
BLINDERS ON

LIVING LIFE AS GOD INTENDED

DR. JULIUS MOSLEY II

CONTENTS

PREFACE

This book is dedicated to all those on this earth and especially those in this country who consider themselves to be "okay" people, who live a good and moral life, and are law-abiding citizens. This book is also dedicated to those who are not such "good" people, who have lived vile lives, and to the One who walked on this earth over two thousand years ago, who made many statements that we all would do well to consider. The Son of God made these statements. Listen to a few: Matt 7:13-17, *"Enter ye in at the strait gate, for wide is the gate, and broad is the way that leadeth to destruction, and many that go in there after. Because strait is the gate and narrow is the way which leadeth unto life, and few there be that find it."*

The Son of God also stated that man should not live by bread alone but by every word that proceeded from His mouth.

Christ again stated in John :37-38, *"If any man thirst, let him come unto me and drink. He that believeth on me, as the scripture hath said, out of his belly shall flow rivers of living water."* The Son of God said that He and the Father were one and that no man can take His life; He can lay it down and pick it up again, meaning that He has eternal existence. He also stated unless you eat of His flesh and drink of His blood, you can have no part of Him. Christ asserted that there were NO GOOD PEOPLE and that only God WAS and IS GOOD!!

To help you and I understand what is beyond the grave, He tells us in Hebrew 9: 27, "and as it appointed unto men once to die, but after this the judgement." So let's be clear that physical death is not the end of it, but rather the beginning of our eternal existence. To not know what is waiting for you and I beyond the grave is...Living life with blinders on... For He has emphatically stated "that it's appointed unto men once to die and after that the JUDGEMENT!!!!!"

This book is dedicated to those who say there is no God... for God says, "Only a fool says in his heart that there is no God." Lastly, this book is dedicated to those church members who think they are in the kingdom but are not. Consider what God says about church members. Christ gave an illustration of a parable of wheat and tares found in Matt 13: 24-30. Listen to this quotation found in Matt

13:24, "ANOTHER PARABLE PUT HE FORTH UNTO THEM SAYING, THE KINGDOM OF HEAVEN IS LIKENED UNTO A MAN WHICH SOWED GOOD SEED IN HIS FIELD. BUT WHILE MEN SLEPT, HIS ENEMY CAME AND SOWED TARES AMONG THE WHEAT, AND WENT HIS WAY. BUT WHEN THE BLADE WAS SPRUNG UP, AND BROUGHT FORTH FRUIT, THEN APPEARED THE TARES ALSO, SO THE SERVANT OF THE HOUSEHOLDER CAME AND SAID UNTO HIM, SIR, DIDST NOT THOU SOW GOOD SEED IN THE FIELD? FROM WHENCE THEN HAS IT TARES?"

He said unto them, an enemy hath done this. The servant said unto

Him, "Wilt thou then that we go and gather them up?" But he said, "Nay; lest while ye gather up the tares, ye root up also the wheat with them. Let both grow together until the harvest; and in the time of the harvest I will say to the reapers, gather ye first the tares, and bind them in bundles to burn them: but gather the wheat into my barn."

This is what He meant about unsaved "church members". He said there are wheat and tares in the church and not to disturb them, for in so doing you may uproot some of the wheat. The angels will separate the wheat from the tares. The scriptures also say the church members who have been exposed to the light for a long time and never responded to that light… great is the darkness! Then there is the wicked one who is able to counterfeit many things. What makes men assume that he has not counterfeited salvation?

This is why the ultimate goal and dedication of this book is to address and help people who may be "living life with blinders on."

CHAPTER I

Who Am I Or Who Are We
"Living Life with Blinders On"

All of us at some time or another have wondered about our existence. As a small child, I would ask myself questions such as:

Question 1: Who am I and who are we? Where did I come from and where did we come from? It was not enough to simply say, "I came from my mother's womb." Well, where did she come from? That question begged for a better answer.

Question 2: What is it that we must know? Obviously, there are consequences for our existence, since people are being born into this world and are just as easily departing this world by death. In fact, I was told that over a million people the world over die every day. None of them returned to answer the question of what is happening beyond the grave. Since the COVID-19 pandemic, over 500,000 people have died. None of us should take it for granted that life here on earth terminates eventually. People who have had an out-of-body experience will tell you a different story. People who have had   a near-death experience will tell you that they saw their life "flash" before their mind's eye in rapid fashion. I experienced this on two occasions—once I almost drowned in a pool, and the second time I was in a car accident traveling over 80 miles an hour. My high school counselor was driving. He lost control of the steering wheel while driving on a highway that was slightly wet and covered in some areas by cut grass. We went airborne. I was a teenager on both occasions, and both times I thought I was dead.

Question 3: What is expected of us? Surely our time on earth is not just a "joy ride" as some people have said. A joy ride is not the answer. Many people say they have enjoyed a full life here on earth (heaven on earth). Others have said it's been hell on earth. Still others have said, "Enjoy life while you can." None of these answers have satisfied me.

Question 4: Where do we get the proper information for questions that beg for true and correct answers? Is it wise to go through life not knowing the consequences of living? How can intelligent beings not know this?

Let's start by saying there is a book written by forty different authors over thousands of years. This book is divided into two major divisions. One is called the Old Testament and the second is called the New Testament. We call this book "Holy Scripture" or "the Holy Bible."

We cannot know the person who created us or who we are unless we read what's revealed to us in this book. The Bible will either exonerate us or convict or condemn us. To have lived on planet earth without knowing anything about what's written on the pages of this book is "living life with blinders on".

This book tells us that it does not matter who you are—your race, color, sex, or whether you are rich or poor—your name is written in another book called the book of life. The other books are called the books of death. These contain the names of every human being that has ever lived. Everyone whose name is in the "books", which will be the majority of humans that have ever lived, will be judged from the "books". These are the ones who lived on earth with "blinders on". Let's pause for a moment.

This book I spoke of earlier is called the Holy Bible. It has sixtysix books within it, and each has chapters and verses. Within the book called 2 Peter, Chapter 1 verses 20–21 say, *"Knowing this first, that no prophecy of the scripture is of any private interpretation. For the prophecy came not in old time by the will of man: but holy men of God spoke as they were moved by the Holy Ghost."*

You may say, "Who is the Holy Ghost?" or "What is the Holy Ghost?" God exists in three persons: God the Father, God the Son, and God the Holy Spirit. These three are one. God the Father is a spirit and is invisible; God the Holy Spirit is a spirit and is invisible; but God the Son is visible like you and I are visible. So God is triune—He exists in three persons but they are one. Confusing? Not really.

Listen carefully. We as human beings created in the image of God are also triune beings. How do we know this? We can't outside of what the scripture reveals to us.

Let's pause for a moment.

In the very first book of the Bible, called Genesis, God tells us this. In verse 7, it says, *"And the Lord God formed man of the dust of the ground and breathed into his nostrils the breath of life, and man became a living soul."*

Listen carefully. When God formed man from "dirt," he had no life. When the breath of God came in contact with the body of man, which lay motionless on the ground, man became a living soul. Listen carefully again: God is spirit and invisible. God's spirit is "life." When His breath came in contact with the visible part of man (man's body), man became a living soul.

Therefore, man is a triune being—being composed of a body that is visible, a soul that is invisible, and a spirit that is also invisible.

One couldn't know this outside of knowing what the Scripture says about man.

That first man's name was Adam, who is the father of the entire human race. Every human being who has ever existed came from that first man, Adam.

Let's pause for a moment.

Let's let the Holy Scriptures tell us further about man. In the same book of Genesis, verses 2:21–23, it says this: *"And the Lord God caused a deep sleep to fall upon Adam and while he slept; he took one of the ribs from Adam's side and closed up the flesh instead thereof, and the rib, which the Lord God had taken from man, made he a woman, and brought her unto the man. And Adam said, 'This is now bone of my bones and flesh of my flesh.' She shall be called woman because she was taken out of man."*

Facts to know: The entire human race is an offspring of these two human beings. No other beings were ever made outside of the birth channel of these two human beings. And no! Man did not evolve from any lower form of life… sorry!

There is a reason for man becoming the way he is today, but that was never the intent of God. Adam and Eve are responsible for that. It stemmed from their disobedience to God and, more in particular, Adam's disobedience of God, because he is the one to whom God had given His command.

Let's pause for a moment.

In Genesis 1:1, God stated that "In the beginning", He "created the heaven and the earth." Essentially, this means, "In the beginning of the creation of man, earth, and everything that dwells thereon." Within everything He created, He placed a seed to reproduce itself. He said, "Be fruitful and multiply." Therefore, Adam reproduced in his likeness other human beings from his wife and mate, Eve. Therefore, all human beings originated from two human beings, making the entire human race brothers and sisters.

Then, what disrupted God's perfect plan? Well, there was an "angel" in heaven that had rebelled against God, along with many others who were kicked out of heaven. How do we know this? From the Holy Scriptures. Consider Isaiah 14:12–14:

> *"How art thou fallen from heaven, O Lucifer, son of the morning!*
> *How art thou cut down to the ground, which didst weaken the nations! For*

thou has said in thine heart, "I will ascend into heaven, I will exalt my

thorne above the status of God: I will also sit upon the moment of the

congregation, in the sides of the north. I will ascend above the height of the

clouds, I will be like the most High."

This Angel was called "the son of the morning"; the wicked one; the devil; the serpent; Lucifer. All are names given by the God who created this angel that rebelled against Him, along with many other angels that are called demons. They are all spirits, but they are dangerous!

Why is this important? It's important because they are present today, destroying human life and wreaking havoc on the people of this earth. Satan is the one that deceived Eve, and Eve in turn convinced her husband to disobey God and brought destruction upon the earth and the human race.

Now, let's take a look at the human race and get an understanding of why our behavior is like it is today. Back to the scriptures again.

Look at Genesis 2:15–16: "*And the Lord took Adam, put him into the garden (a place of heavenly bliss) of Eden, to dress it and keep it. And the Lord God commanded Adam, saying, of every tree of the Garden thou mayest freely eat...but the tree of knowledge of good and evil; thou shall not eat of it; for the day that Thou eatest thereof thou shall surely die.*" Now listen to what happened in Genesis 3:1–13:

"Now the serpent was more subtitle than any beast of the field which

the Lord God had made. And he said unto the woman, Yea, hath God

said, ye shall not eat of every tree of the garden?...and the woman said to the

serpent, we may eat of the fruit of the trees of the garden: But of the fruit of the tree which is in the midst of the garden, God hast said, we shall not eat of it, neither shall ye touch it, lest you die. And the serpent said unto the woman, ye shall not surely die. For God doth know that in the day ye eat thereof, then your eyes shall be opened, and ye shall be as gods, knowing good and evil. And when the woman saw that the tree was good for food, and that was it was pleasant to the eyes and a tree to be desired to make one wise, she took of the fruit thereof, and did eat, and gave also unto her husband with her; and he did eat. And the eyes of both them were opened, and they knew that were naked; and they sewed fig leaves together, and made themselves aprons. And they heard the voice of the Lord God walking in the garden in the cool of the day; and Adam and his wife hid themselves from the presence of the Lord God amongst the trees of the garden. And the Lord God called unto Adam, and said unto him, Where Art Thou? And he said, I heard thou voice in the garden, and I was afraid, because I was naked; and I hid myself. And he said, who told you that you wast naked? Hast thou eaten of the tree, where I commanded thee that thou shouldest not eat? And the man said, the woman whom thou gavest to be with me, she gave me of the tree, and I did eat.

"And the Lord God said unto the woman, what is this that thou hast done? And the woman said, the serpent beguiled me, and I did eat. Therefore the Lord God cursed the serpent, the woman Eve, and her husband, Adam."

Listen carefully. Verse 14 says, *"And the Lord God said unto the serpent, Because there hast done this, thou are cursed above all cattle and above every beast of the field; upon thy belly shall thou go, and dust shalt thou eat all the days of thy life."*

Question I: Do snakes crawl on their bellies today? Is the curse still in effect today? Yes!

Listen to a very key statement:

Verse 15: *And I will put enmity between thee and the woman, and between thy seed and her seed; it shall bruise thy head and thou shall bruise his heel.*

Curse to the woman:

Unto the woman he said, I will greatly multiply thy sorrow and thy conception; in sorrow thou shalt bring forth children, and thy desire shall be to thy husband and he shall rule over thee.

Question II: Do women have birth pains during childbirth? Do women seek to control men today? Is the curse still in effect today? Yes!

Curse to the man:

Verse 17: *And unto Adam he said, "Because thou hast hearken to the voice of thy wife and hast eaten of the tree of which I commanded thee saying, thou shalt not eat of it: cursed is the ground for thy sake; in sorrow shalt thou eat of it all the days of thy life. Thorns and thistles shall it bring forth to thee and thou shall eat the herbs of the field. In the sweat of thy face shalt thou eat bread, till thou return unto the ground; for out of it wast thou taken: for dust thou art and unto dust shall thou return."*

Question III: Do men have to make a living by the sweat of their brow? Do men grow old and die? Is the curse still in effect today? Yes!

Question IV: Can you now begin to understand why the world is the way it is today? Can you begin to understand why men and women, boys and girls are the way they are today? Yes—we are living in bodies that have been cursed! No good thing can come from a cursed body. In Scripture, God calls that body by many names: lump of clay, vessel, temple, tabernacle, body of death, et cetera.

God is holy. We are unholy. We have been cursed, and there is no cursed thing going to heaven. Let me state that again: There is no cursed thing going to *Heaven…only that which is perfect! God is perfect, sinless, undefiled, and holy!*

Perhaps now you and I can understand why we cannot solve our own problems… because *we are the problem!*

CHAPTER II

What We Must Know

We all are descendants of Adam. We were in the genes of Adam— the entire human race.

Remember, God said, "Be fruitful and multiply." Before the foundation of the earth, God had already determined when you and I would be born, whether we would be male or female, and how our vessel would look; what we do know is whatever that vessel turned out to be, it would be a cursed vessel/body because of our heritage from our first parents, Adam and Eve.

Remember, God formed man from the dust of the earth. While the body/dust lay on the ground, it was lifeless. When God (who is life) breathed the breath of life into the nostril of the body, his breath came in contact with the body and man became a living soul.

Now, why is this important to understand?

It's important to understand because it's the reason that the vast majority of human beings go through life with blinders on!

Let's examine this triune body of man: body, soul, and spirit. The body gives us the ability to relate to the environment: other people, nature, and things. The scripture tells us and we know for a fact that the life of the body is in the blood (see Revelation 17:11). The fleshy body is the material part of us, which will grow old and die from either disease, crime, old age, or all manner of other factors. When the blood stops flowing within your body, you are dead! Now remember, God also called the body a vessel. The vessel is instructed by the soul. The vessel is what we move around in. There are small vessels, tall vessels, fat vessels, skinny vessels, and vessels of many colors—black, white, brown, yellow, et cetera. A vessel is a vessel and nothing else. These vessels man has called races. But remember, God says in Romans 2:11, For there is no respect of persons with God. "no respect of vessels." He created all of them for His glory, but man tries to make vessels different. That's the curse!

Now let's give an example of the value to God of the vessel, when we try to please Him with it. Suppose you visited my home on a very hot day. You had been working, sweating, or just playing, and you became very thirsty. You asked me for a cool glass of water. I went to my kitchen and took a glass out of my dirty sink that had greasy fingerprints on it, lipstick marks around the rim, and leftover crumbs from a previous meal stuck to it. Then I filled it up to the brim with some nice cool water from the refrigerator and handed it to you. Would you drink it? No, you wouldn't. Not because of the water, but because of the dirty glass! That's how God looks at every vessel, because it's been cursed! Get the picture? You cannot please God with your body/vessel. It doesn't matter how you dress it up, what pious position you put it in, or what kind of work you do with it. It's still a cursed vessel and will remain that way until you die! We all must remember that the body is but a vessel. You and I did not determine what vessel we would be born in …whether a male or female vessel. We had no say as to whether we would be born a white vessel, a black vessel, a brown vessel, a yellow vessel etc. We had no say as to whether our parents would be rich or poor; educated or uneducated. What God did tell us was not to think of your self more highly than you ought to. To think that the vessel you were born in makes you superior than anyone else is living life with blinders on…FOR THERE IS NO RESPECT OF PERSON WITH GOD. He also stated that everyone must stand before God to give an account for everything you and I have done while in the body. We also do well to remember that body we are in will return back to dust, the soul and spirit shall return to God to be judged. Therefore, remember the body maybe colored, but the soul is COLORLESS. To treat a person on the basis of their color….is living life with blinders on.

Now let's look at the soul. It has all of the attributes needed for the body. It's where the real person resides. It houses the mind, will, and emotions. It tells the body what to do. Listen to this voice from the scripture:

"There was a certain rich man, which was clothed in purple and fine linen, and fared sumptuously every day. There was a certain beggar named Lazarus, which was laid at his gate full of sores and desired to be fed with the crumbs which fell from the rich man's table; more over the dogs came and licked his sores. And it came to pass that the beggar died, and was carried by the angels into Abraham's bosom; the rich man died also and was buried. And in hell he lifted up his eyes, being in torments and seeing Abraham afar off, and Lazarus in his bosom. And he cried and said, Father Abraham, have mercy on me, and send Lazarus, that he may dip the tip of his finger in water, and cool my tongue, for I am tormented in this flame. But Abraham said, son, remember that there in thy lifetime receivedst

thy good things, and likewise Lazarus evil things: but now he is comforted, and thou art tormented. And beside all this, between us and you there is a great gulf fixed: so that they which would pass from hence to you cannot; neither can they pass to us, that would come from thence. Then he said, I pray thee therefore Father, that thou wouldest send him to my father's house; for I have five brethren; that he may testify unto them, lest they also came into this place of torment. Abraham saith unto him, they are Moses and the prophets; let them hear them. And he said, Nay, Father Abraham; but if one went unto them from the dead, they will repent. …And he said unto him, if they hear not Moses and the prophets, neither will they be persuaded through one rose from the dead." (Luke 16:19–31)

Notice that the soul of the rich man lifted up his eyes—clearly the soul can see; further, the soul cried and was tormented… so the soul has emotion. The rich man said he had five brothers back on earth and wished them not to experience what he was experiencing… so the soul has a memory. He wanted not for his brothers to come to that awful place… so the soul can make decisions. Therefore, in the soul resides all of the elements for existence, mind, emotion, and will… it's the decision portion of man, which is invisible, but also cursed. Remember: living life with blinders on!

It is extremely important that we understand the element of the soul. The soul is invisible, on the inside of the body. Listen to God tells us in Ephesian 6:10 -17, *Finally, my brethren, be strong in the Lord, and in the power of His might. Put on the whole armor of God, that ye may be able to stand against the wiles of the devil. For we wrestle not against flesh blood, but against flesh and blood, but against principalities, against powers, against the rulers of the darkness of this world, against spiritual wickedness in high places. Wherefore take unto you the whole armor of God, that ye may be able to withstand in the evil day, and having done all, to stand. Stand therefore, having your loins girt about the truth and having on the breastplate of righteousness; and your feet shod with the preparation of the gospel of peace; above all, taking the shield of faith, wherein ye shall able to quench all the fiery darts of the wicked. And take the helmet of salvation, and the sword of the spirit, which is the word of God.*

Now for the spirit. In the spirit resides conscience, intuition, and worship. Remember how the serpent told Eve that if she ate the fruit from the tree of knowledge, she would be like God, having the ability to know the difference between good and evil? Well, the result of that action left you and I with a conscience to know the difference between right and wrong. It's like a pendulum on a clock that swings back and forth—right, wrong, right, wrong. It doesn't argue with us, debate with us, or discuss anything with us. It just tells us what we are about to do is either right or wrong. Because the spirit has been cursed also, our tendency is to overrule our conscience and do whatever we want to do. Then there is intuition—haven't you been in a place that you felt you had been before when you never had? Haven't you observed something or walked into a meeting and within yourself known that something was not right there? Or when you're somewhere and although you can't see anything wrong you just know that there is "no good happening" there? Part of the curse!

The other feature of the spirit is the ability to worship. This is the only thing the spirit does that we cannot control. Listen to this verse of scripture found in the book of John. Listen to what the Samaritan woman said to the Son of God in verses 19–24:

"The woman saith unto Christ, Sir I perceive that thou art a prophet. Our fathers worshiped in this mountain and ye say, that in Jerusalem is the

place men ought to worship Jesus answered and said unto her woman, believe me, the hour cometh, when ye shall neither in this mountain, nor yet in Jerusalem worship the Father; ye worship ye know not what: we know what we worship: for salvation is of the Jews. But the hour cometh, and Now is when the true worshipers will worship the father in SPIRIT and in Truth; For the Father seeth such to worship Him. God is a spirit; and they that worship Him must worship Him in SPIRIT and in Truth."

In other words, you must have the spirit of God in you that is alive… but because our spirit has been cursed, you and I do not have the ability to commune with the true and living God. Nevertheless, we do have a spirit even though we're cursed. The spirit within us gives us the ability to worship. However, being cursed, we will worship the god of this world, who is Satan. Satan encourages us to worship ourselves, one another, things, animals, cars, homes, jobs, politicians, actors, athletes, celebrities, parents, siblings, education, achievements, and the list goes on!

Let's pause for a moment. Remember the curse that took place in the garden? Well, God cursed the creation as well. In Genesis 3:17, it says, *"And unto Adam God said, because thou hast harken to thy wife and has eaten of the tree of which I commanded thee, saying, thou shalt not eat of it: CURSED is the ground FOR THY SAKE. Do grass, flowers, trees, plants die and shed their leaves and limbs? Do all lower form of animals die also?"*

When Adam sinned against God, along with his wife, Eve, Satan took over ownership of the human race. Listen to what God says in 2 Corinthians 4:3–4: *"But if our gospel is hid, it is hid to them that are lost in whom the god of this world has blinded the minds of those that are lost."*

Satan owns the world and everything that's in it. Consider another verse of scripture, Matthew 4:1. *"Then was the Son of God led up of the spirit into the wilderness to be tempted of the devil."* From verses 1 to 11, listen at verses 8 and 9.

"Again, the devil taketh him up into an exceeding high mountain, and showeth him all the KINGDOMS of the world and the glory of them, and saith to him, all these things will I give thee, if you will fall down and worship me."

Now tell me who owns *all the governments of this world…* Satan, of course! Now, you want to know why all the governments of this world are corrupt? There is nothing wrong with the governments. What makes the governments so hard and dishonest? It's the people/ leaders that run the government.

But God said about leaders: "the people get who they deserve"! Why is that? Because the people are just as corrupt as the leaders! What you need to understand about Satan is that he is a fallen angel, created by God, who rebelled against God, tried to be like God, and attempted to overthrow God's kingdom; cast out of heaven, he is a spirit who has taken control of this world, and he has a goal of defeating God's prized possession—man! Listen to what God says about him in John 10:10: *"The thief cometh not, but for to steal, to kill, and to destroy."*

That is exactly what Satan does today. He uses his skills to address man's fallen (cursed) nature; thusly causing man to try to live life on earth without regard for "God's authority." Listen what God says in Matthew 10:28: *"Fear not him who is able to kill the body, but rather fear him who is able to kill both body and soul and cast into Hell's fire"!*

Listen to what God has to say about our fallen nature in Roman 1:18–23: *"For the wrath of God is revealed from heaven against all ungodliness and unrighteousness of men, who hold the truth in unrighteousness, because that which may be known of God is manifest in them; for God has showed it unto them. For the invisible things of him from the creation of the world are clearly seen, being understood by the things that are made, even his eternal power and Godhead, so they are without excuse."*

Surely you can see that birds fly in the air, day follows night, men walk upright with eyes, nose, ears, hands, and feet all in the same place on our bodies, indicating that there has to be a master designer far superior than we are. The thing that's made cannot be greater than the one that made it… common sense, right?

Let's continue with verse 21: *"Because that, when they knew God, they glorified not as God, neither were they thankful but being vain in their imagination, and their foolish heart was darken. Professing themselves to be wise, they became fools. And changed the glory of the uncorruptible God into an image made like corruptible man, and to birds, and four-footed beasts and creeping things."*

Idols. Observe how our international brothers and sisters use burning candles, oranges, and bogotas that they light, along withincense; notice the soothsayers, palmists, hand readers, others using candles, having commune parties, et cetera.

Verse 24 says, *"Wherefore God also gave them up to uncleanness through the lusts of their own hearts, to dishonor their own bodies between themselves who changed the truth of God into a lie, and they worshiped and served the creature more than the creator."*

Lovers of pets and other animals—dogs, cats, reptiles, lions, tigers, monkeys—often treat them better than they do human beings. Some people have taken the love for dogs to a level we have never seen in this country before. There are dog and cat hospitals, even cemeteries. Some have even included these animals in their wills. What a travesty. Our fallen nature causes people to place a greater priority on dogs than human life (another example of living life with blinders on).

As a result, God has also given them up to uncleanliness through the lusts of their own hearts to dishonor their own bodies between themselves who change the truth of God into a lie, and worshipped and served the creature more than the creator who is blessed forever. Amen. For this cause, God gave them up unto vile affections; for even their women did change the natural use into that which is against nature…LGBT community, et cetera.

And likewise, the men leaving the natural use of women, burned in their lust for one another; men with men working that which is unseemly and receiving in themselves that recompense of their error—all kinds of venereal diseases, AIDS, et cetera, homosexuality, bisexuality, et cetera. And even as they did not like to retain God in their knowledge, God gave them over to a reprobate mind (a mind that cannot distinguish right from wrong (very serious state of being) to do these things that are not convenient; being filled with all unrighteousness, fornication, wickedness, full of envy, debate malignantly whispers backbiters, haters of God, despiteful, proud, boasters, inventors of evil things, disobedient to parents (killing parents), without understanding (scholarly opinions, discussions, theories, workshops, self-help group sessions) covenant breakers, without natural affections, implacable, unmerciful, who knowing the judgment of God that they which commit such things are worthy of death. Not only do the same but have pleasure in them that do them.

Therefore, thou are inexcusable, on man, whosoever thou are that judgest; for wherein thou judgest another, thou condemnest thyself, for that thou judgest doest the same thing. But we are sure that the judgement of God is according to truth against them which judgest such things. And thinks thou this, o man that judgest them which do such things, and does the same things, that thou shall escape the judgement of God? Or despiseth thou the riches of His goodness and forebearance and long suffering; not knowing that the goodness of God leadeth thee to repentance?

But after thou hardness and impenitent heart treasures up to thyself wrath again the day of wrath and revelation of the righteousness of God versus who will render to every man according to his deeds. To them who by patient continuance in well doing seek for glory and honor and immortality, eternal life. But unto them that are contentious and do not obey the truth, but obey unrighteousness, indignation and wrath, tribulation and anguish, upon every soul of man that doeth evil, of the Jew first and also of the Gentile. But glory, honor and peace to every man that worketh good, to the Jew first, and also to the Gentile: for there IS NO RESPECT OF PERSONS WITH GOD.

Pause for a moment. Now we just mentioned two new groups of people. Why is this important?

Listen to me well.

There are only two races of people in this world: Jews and Gentiles. Nothing else! You are either a Jew or a Gentile. When was this started and why is it important to know?

Well, God is a covenant-making God. We must go back to the beginning to understand this because it's another reason you may be living life with blinders on!

Listen to these verses from Genesis 12:1. The call by God to Abram: *"Now the Lord said to Abram, get thee out of thy country, and from thy kindred, and from thou father's house, unto a land I will show thee and I will make of thee a great nation, and I will bless thee, and make thy name great, and thou shall be a blessing; and I will bless them that bless thee, and curse them that curseth thee, and in thee shall ALL FAMILIES OF THE world BE BLESSED"* (emphasis added).

So Abram (who later God named "Abraham") departed as the Lord had spoken unto him. God later called him the "Father of Faith" because he didn't question God, but simply obeyed. That's what God expects of ALL OF US!

But what is great about this is that God is a God that keeps His promises. He is a God that cannot LIE. That's why you and I have hope— for LATER the Son of God said, "I and the Father are one and whatever the Father does, so do I for I came from the Father; for I am in the Father and the Father is in Me." Powerful statements.

We will expound later.

Let's look at some facts so we don't continue to "live life with blinders on".

Fact One: There are two invisible kingdoms on this earth—the kingdom of God and the kingdom of Satan. There are more people on earth in the kingdom of Satan than in the kingdom of God. How do I know? Because God says so! If you have spiritual eyes, you are able to agree with God.

Fact Two: There are two races of people on this earth: Jews and Gentiles.

Fact Three: All humans are born into the kingdom of Satan, which is called the Kingdom of Darkness, the sinful kingdom. Listen to this in Psalms 58:3: *"The wicked are estranged from the womb; they go astray as soon as they be born, speaking lies."*

You don't have to teach a baby to lie. They are born with that ability. Consider another verse from Psalm 51:5: *"I was shapen in iniquity and in sin did my mother conceive me."*

LISTEN to another truth in Romans 5:12: *"Wherefore as by one man (Adam) sin entered the world, and death by sin; so death passed upon all men, for that all have sinned."*

And further in Roman 3:10–18: *"As it is written, there is none righteous, No NOT ONE, There is none that understandest, there is none that sleekest after God. They are all gone out of the way, They are together become unprofitable, there is none that doeth Good, no, not one. Their throat is an open sepulcher; with their tongues they have used deceit, the poison asps is under their lips; whose mouth is full of cursing and bitterness. Their feet are swift to shed blood destruction and misery are in their ways, And the way of peace they have not known there is no fear of God before their eyes, Now we know that what things so ever the law saith, it saith to them that are under the law (Law of God): that every mouth may be stopped, and all the world may become GUILTY BEFORE GOD!"*

(Emphasis added.)

Now going back to the two races as mentioned before, based upon the promise that God made to Abraham, the descendants of Abraham are God's chosen people (the Jews). Listen to what God says in Romans 4:3: *"For what saith the scripture? Abraham believed God and it was counted unto him for righteousness."*

Listen carefully. Not all Jews who consider themselves Jews are true Jews. Only the descendants of Abraham, Isaiah, and Jacob are true Jews. Why is this important again? It's because God made a promise to Abraham that through him all the families of the earth would be blessed. Remember also back in the garden when God pronounced the curse against the serpent (Satan) in verse 3:14: *"And the Lord God said unto the serpent, Because thou hast done this, thou are cursed above all cattle, and above every beast of the field; upon they belly shalt thou go, and dust shalt though eat all the days of thy life. And I will put enmity between thee and the woman, and between thy seed and her seed."* [Listen well. Her "seed," not her and Adam's seed] a woman will give birth to a child without the (involvement of a man's seed) sometime in the (Genesis 3:15) it shall bruise thy head, and thou shall bruise his heel. Now which is the most devasting blow—to the head or to the heel?

Let's go back to observe another fact.

Men and women, boys and girls, live a very comfortable life here on earth, don't you agree? Everybody goes about their daily activities and routines, going to work, to school, trying to obtain degrees to get a better-paying jobs, such that one could enjoy an even greater life; getting married and raising families; taking vacations, participating in organizations for self-fulfillment; attending church; celebrating achievements; awarding one another; achieving great things in sports; being paid high salaries; enjoying luxurious lifestyles; becoming CEOs of banks; entertainers having great lifestyles, Academy Awards, esteemed award shows with high "dress-down" appearances, lots of laughter and accolades, attending churches to add to a well-rounded life; becoming community leaders—city councilmen, mayors, governors, senators, representatives, presidents, supreme court justices, high-profile attorneys, newscasters with interesting local and worldwide news, college professors, policemen, foremen, and the list goes on. But not to leave out the law breakers, the criminals. The only problem with this is that most of us "live life with blinders on".

To ignore what our creator has said is extremely dangerous. Listen to what He has said in Hebrews 9:27: *"And as it is appointed unto men once to die, but after that the judgement."*

Remember we talked about man being a triune man—being made of body, soul, and spirit. Well, this is when you really find that out. Nevertheless, the wise person should want to find this out before he dies.

Physical death is just the beginning, not the end. Physical death is a part of the curse on man. Remember, "dust thou art and dust thou shall return" was a curse given to Adam (your parent and the head of the human race), all because of disobedience to God. Well, so have we disobeyed. Every man, woman, and child must give account for what they did while living in this body.

Remember, there is none righteous, no not one, but God is a sinless, righteous judge. When an unrighteous person dies, his body returns to dust, but his soul and spirit are cast into a place called Hades or outer darkness, where there is weeping and gnashing of teeth. It is a holding place where people wait for the final judgment. There are billions down there waiting; some you knew and some you don't know. Then there are some who died who are with the LORD Jesus right now, who will be judged only to determine what eternal awards they will receive based on how they lived and what they did or didn't do after becoming a member of the body of Christ, the head of the "second human race."

You did know that there are two human races on earth; one human race is where Adam is the head and the last Adam (who is Christ) is head of the second human race. I will explain this later.

There is a second death for the soul and spirit. This is the eternal death. Read carefully the book of Revelation (last book of the Bible). Revelation 20:10–15 John, one of the apostles of Christ, was given this information in a vision. *"And the devil that deceived man was cast into the lake of fire and brimstone, where the beast and the false prophet are, and shall be tormented day and night for ever and ever. And I saw a great white throne and him that sat on it, from whose face the earth and heaven fled away; and there was found no place for them (to hide). And I saw the dead, small and great."* Well-known people, average people, good people (by man's standards) poor people, kings, presidents, rulers, homeless people, some church people, et cetera.

Stand before God; and the books were opened; and another book was opened, which is the book of life. Remember I told you earlier that every person that has ever lived has their name in a book and the dead (those who never got their names out of the "books", who never got out of Adam's family through ignorance or unwillingness), were judged out of those things (your life) which were in the books, according to their works (how they lived, ignoring the authority of God; living for self). "And the sea gave up the dead which were in it" (it doesn't matter how you died physically, or whether you were burned, cremated, etc., you are coming back into those same bodies to be judged, for nothing is too hard for God).

Remember those that died with "blinders on" who went to outer darkness where there was weeping and gnashing of teeth? That's the place called death and hell. Death and hell delivered up the dead which were in them; and they were judged every man according to their works. And death and hell were cast into the lake of fire. This is the second death. Remember, the first death was a physical death… death of the body. The second death is all of the triune man (body, soul, and spirit). "And whosoever was not found written in the "book of life" was cast into the lake of fire." This is for eternity—no other opportunities—you will burn "forever"!

In Revelation 21:1, look what John saw. "And I saw a new heaven and a new earth; for the first heaven and earth were passed away; and there was no more sea." Continue to read the rest of these chapters for yourself and you will be greatly blessed. I have one other thing to share with you, then I will tell you how to get out of this dilemma and leave the family of Adam to get into the family of God and live life eternally with God!

Remember we talked about man having a triune body, made in the image of the triune God. God the Father is invisible (Spirit); God the Holy Spirit, who is invisible. But God the Son is visible, whose name is Jesus.

Man's body is visible and called flesh and bones; man's soul is invisible and also called "flesh" or "self" (by God), and man's spirit is invisible. Now we know that God said that flesh and bones cannot enter into heaven. Listen to John 6:63: *"It is the spirit that quickenth; the flesh profiteth nothing."* Trying to please God through the energy of your flesh (soul) is fruitless.

Listen to another apostle, Paul, in Romans 7:1. Paul talks about the law of God, trying to be a good person by keeping the law: *"Know ye not, brethren [for I speak to them that know the law] how that the law hath dominion [control] over a man as long as he liveth." Verse 14 says, "For we know that the law is spiritual; but I am carnal, sold under sin. For that which I do I allow not: for what I would that do I not; but what I hate, that I do. If then I do that which I would not I consent unto the Law [of God] that it is good. Now then it is not more I [self] that do it, but sin [curse] that dwelleth in me." Verse 18 says, "For I know that in me (that is in my flesh [self]) dwelleth no good thing; for to will [want to] is present with me; but how to perform that which is good I find not. For the good that I would I do not; but evil which I would not, that I do. Now if I do that I would not, it is no more I that do it, but sin [curse] that dwelleth in me. I find then a law, that, when I would do good, evil is present with me for I delight in the law of God after the inward man [spirit]. But I see another law in my members [eyes, arms, legs, hand feet…all of the things that hang off your physical body] warring against the law of my mind, and bringing me into captivity to the law of sin which is in my members."* Finally, listen to what Paul says out of exacerbation: "O wretched man that I am, who shall deliver me from this body of death?" This is what we all say because we are living out the curse!

Now, do you want to know where racism, bigotry, hatred, deceit, jealousy, envy, pride, arrogance, self-pity, lack of self-worth, feelings of superiority, thinking one race is better than another, cheating, adultery, and living a lifestyle unacceptable to God came from? The "soul," which has been cursed!

When tragic world events that are performed and orchestrated by the "god of this world" happen, we often hear people on TV and other media outlets, such as Google, Facebook, Twitter, and TikTok, use the expression, "Keep the faith." What faith? Whose faith?

Those words have no meaning. Man's faith means that if you believe "hard enough," it will happen. That is not faith; that's foolishness. Faith must have a belief in someone or something; a reliance on a person who cannot lie. A belief in a person who is immutable. A belief in a person who never sleeps. There is only one person that would fit that description! You must first believe in God and that He is a rewarder of them who diligently seek Him. Psalm 53:1 says, *The fool says in his heart there is no God.*

True faith is very important. Listen to the scriptural response to faith in Hebrew 11:6. "But without faith it is IMPOSSIBLE to please God; for he that cometh to God must believe he exists and that HE is a rewarder of them that diligently seek him" (emphasis added).

What about these human expressions: "We will pray for you," or "Our prayers are with you."

Pray to "who"? Listen to what God has to say about praying. "My eyes are not blind that I can't see you, my ears are not dull that I can't hear you, my arms are not short that I can't reach you, but your sins have hidden you from me."

Isaiah 50:1: *"Behold the Lord's hand is not shortened that it cannot save; neither his ear hard that he cannot hear; But your sins have separated between you and your God, and your sins have hid his face from you, that he will not hear."*

Another example of "living life with blinders on" is one's false assumptions about one's relationship with God. Your soul is what God called the flesh. This is the source of all sin because this is where knowledge is retained, beliefs are stored (memory), decisions are made (willpower), and actions are initiated, whether they are good or bad. The body is what feeds the soul, either from the eye gate, the ear gate, or the taste and feel gates, which are all from man's physical senses and all are being controlled by the "god of this world," the prince of darkness. Trying to get to God through your physical senses or even please God through your physical senses is fruitless. Remember, God is a spirit and therefore one must use the spirit part of himself to interact with God. Some would say that God spoke to them and gave them instructions to do "this and that." God can't speak to a spirit that is cursed and dead!

The soul/flesh has a problem with God. Listen carefully to this verse found in Romans 8:5: *"For they that are after the flesh (live life in the flesh) do mind the things of the flesh… for to be carnally minded is enmity [deep hatred] against God; for it is not subject to the Law of God, neither indeed can be."* Verse 8 says they that are in the flesh "cannot please God."

So, to man, one may appear to be a good and respectable person who takes care of his family, does charitable work within his community, saves the animals, and even has animals at home that are very well cared for, has good kids, stays out of trouble, votes in elections, attends church, has a good education, came from a good and respectable family, et cetera. Then there is the other soul/person who is just the opposite: a disrespectful law breaker who steals, kills, irresponsibly has children out of wedlock, is destructive, and influences kids to do likewise.

But listen to what God says about both of these people in Romans 3:23. "All have sinned and fallen short of the Glory of God." Romans 3:10 states, "As it is written, there is none righteous, no not one. There is none that understandeth, there is none that seeketh after God. They are all gone out of the way, they are together become unprofitable; there is none that doeth good, no not one. A person cannot be helped until he realizes that he needs help." Listen, all of our righteousness is like " filthy rags in God's sight" (Isaiah 64:6).

When we as a people look at one another through our moralist eyes, we appear to be pretty good people. But we must view ourselves as God views us. He is the potter and we are the clay. Listen to what God says in Roman 9:13–24: *"As it is written, Jacob have I loved, but Esau have I hated." Esau sold his birthright to Jacob for a bowl of soup.*

"What shall we say then? Is there unrighteousness in God? God forbid for God saith to Moses

"I will have mercy on whom I will have mercy and I will have compassion on whom I will have compassion. So then it is not of him that willeth, nor of him that runneth, but of God that showeth mercy. For the scripture said unto Pharaoh [who held the Israelites in slavery] even for this same purpose have I raised thee up, that I might show my power in thee, and that my name be declared throughout all the earth. Therefore haith he mercy on who he will have mercy and on who he will he hardeth. Thou wilt say there unto me, why doth he yet find fault? For Who hath resisted his will? Nay but old man, who not thou that repliest against God? shall the thing formed say to him that formed it, why hast though made me thus? Hath not the potter power over the clay, of the same lump to make one vessel with honor, and another to dishonor? What if God, willing to show his wealth, and to make his power known, endureth with much suffering the vessels of wrath fitted for destruction:

and that he might make known the riches of his Glory on the vessels of mercy, which he had afore prepared unto glory. Even us, who he hated called, not of the Jews only but also of the Gentiles?"

I hope by now you understand that what we consider a normal lifestyle is unacceptable to God. No matter whether you are a perfect citizen, a murderer, a thief, or whether you are rich or poor, in the sight of God we are all sinners and as we are reminded in Romans 6:23: *"…the wages of sin is death."* Don't get so comfortable in whatever state you find yourself. Your body, soul, and spirit have been cursed!

Listen again to what God says in Hebrews 10:31: *"It's a fearful thing to fall unto the hands of the Living God."* And in Hebrews 4:13: *"Neither is there any creature that is not manifest in his sight; But all things are naked and opened unto the eyes of him with whom we have to do."* So, wake up, folks. Let's get those "blinders off our eyes."

Listen closely. Isaiah 55:6–9 says, *"Seek ye the Lord while he may be found, call ye upon him while he is near: Let the wicked forsake his way, and the unrighteous man his thoughts: and let him return unto the Lord, and he will have mercy upon him; and to our God and he will have mercy upon him; for he will abundantly pardon. For my thoughts are not your thoughts, neither are your ways my ways saith the Lord. For as the heavens are higher than the earth. So are my ways higher than your ways and my thoughts higher than your thoughts."*

Pause. What then must people do to have the "blinders" removed from their eyes?

You begin by believing and trusting God and what he says. Remember, our thoughts are not his thoughts. Let's not forget that the Word of God is written down in sixty-six books of the Bible— written by over forty different authors chosen by God and moved by the third person of the God Head (the Holy Spirit).

Pause. Why is the Bible, the Word of God, so significant? Because we need to hear it.

What we have been hearing for the most part is television and other media forms, as well as people we trust, all of which are tools of Satan—news media, social media, schools (elementary, junior high, high school, and college)—all owned by Satan. He uses these tools to damage our thinking and keep us blinded from the truth.

Listen to what God says about His Word in Hebrews 4:12:

"For the word of God is quick and powerful, and sharper than any two edged sword, piercing even to the dividing asunder of SOUL and SPIRIT, and of the joints and marrow, and is a discerner of the thoughts and intent of the heart" (emphasis added).

In Psalms 119:105, it says, *"Thy word is a lamp unto my feet and a light unto my pathway."* You and I could never know the mind of God aside from the Word of God. In order for you and me to get out of this body of death, to get your name out of the "books of death" and into "the book of life," and to get out of the family we were born into (the family where Adam is the head) and get into the last Adam (the Son of God—Christ) who is the head of the second human race… you must be born again!

Listen to the Word of God in John 3:1. *"There was a man of the Pharisee [a highly intellectual, learned person – very religious] named Nicodemus, a Ruler of the Jews." Verse 2 says, "The same came to Jesus by night and said unto him, 'Rabbi, we know that thou are a teacher came from God; for no man can do these miracles that thou doest except God be with him.' And Jesus answered and said unto him, 'Verily, verily, I say unto thee, except a man be born again, he cannot see the Kingdom of God.'" Verse 4 says, "Nicodemus saith unto him, 'How can a man be born when he is old? Can he enter the second time into his mother's womb and be born?' Jesus answered and said, "Verily, verily, I say unto thee, except a man be born of water and of the Spirit he cannot enter into the Kingdom of God.'" Verse 6 says, "That which is born of the flesh is flesh; and that which is born of the spirit is spirit. Marvel not that I said unto thee, ye must be born again."*

Now the answer is very clear…have you been born again or have you just been attending church? Are you Christian, Catholic, Jehovah's Witness, Seventh Day Adventist, Mormon, Buddhist, Mason, or any other religious order? It doesn't matter what you professed to be, or if you're an atheist. If you have not been born again, you are yet in your sins headed to the lake of fire to spend an eternity there. Don't deceive yourself. Physical death is not the end, it is just the beginning of an eternity in the lake of fire!

Jew or Gentile, the fate will be the same if you have not been born again. God has no respect of person. Listen again, the Jews are God's chosen people because of the promise God made to Abraham.

Listen to what God says when he speaks of the Jews who are looking for a Messiah to come and rule over them, not recognizing that He has already come and gone back to Heaven. His name was Jesus.

"I say then, have they [Jews] stumbled that they should fall? God forbid; but rather through their fall salvation is come unto the Gentiles for to

provoke the Jews to jealousy. Now if the fall be the riches of the world and the diminishing of them the riches of the Gentiles; how much more their fullness." (Romans 11:11)

Verse 25 says, *"For I would not brethren that ye should be ignorant of this mystery, lest ye should be wise in your own conceits; that blindness in part is happened to Israel until the fullness of the Gentiles be come in."*

Listen folks, that time is fast approaching, for at this time Gentiles have literally turned from God. They try to compete with God; to find solutions to things only God can do.

People are being murdered all over the world—Jews and Gentiles, blacks and whites, young and old, church members and nonchurch members. There are storms and tornadoes, fires caused by lightning, wicked leaders in government; discrimination, drug wars, killing of innocent people, climate changes, et cetera. God has either initiated it or allowed it to happen…just to get our attention and save as many that desire to be saved.

CHAPTER III

Where Is This Information Obtained (And What Must We Do With It?)

We have been instructed as to how we should live. There is an instruction book that holds all of the answers about human beings. It starts from the creation of mankind. To go through life not ever reading or getting an understanding of the words written in that book will be eternally devastating. This book is holy, and the author of this book is holy. There are many books that have been written in an attempt to challenge what's written in the Holy Scriptures, but they have failed miserably. Many religions have been created as a result of the writings of these books.

God says that we are to live by faith and not by sight. He states further that without faith it is impossible to please Him. In the Hebrews 11:6, it states, "But without faith it is impossible to please him; for he that cometh to God must believe that he is [exists] and that he is a rewarder of those that diligently seek him." In Hebrews 12:2, it states, *"Looking unto Jesus the author and finisher of our faith; who for the joy that was set before him endureth the cross, despising the shame, and is set down at the right hand of the throne of God."* Hopefully, now you understand why we must live by faith and not by sight. To live by faith requires the use of your mind but to live by sight requires the use of your physical senses, which in this world is extremely dangerous.

It's dangerous because God tells us that the god of this world has blinded the minds of those that "believe not" what He says. This is found in 2 Corinthians 4: 3-4: *"In whom the god of this world hath blinded the minds of those which believe not…"*

We were also told to be in the world but not "of" the world, and that Satan was like a roaring lion going to and fro throughout the earth seeking whom he may devour. He does it by controlling us through our physical senses…our eyes, ears, mouth, nose, and sense of feel. People in the world don't recognize that we live in two worlds—the physical and the spiritual. The physical world is obvious to you and me. It's the spiritual world that is not. But God warns us that our battles are not against flesh and blood.

> ***"Put on the whole armor of God [the Word of God— Holy Bible] that ye may be able to stand against the wiles of the devil… for we wrestle not against flesh and blood [people], but against principalities [organized satanic beings, demons] against powers, against rulers… the rulers of the darkness of this world, against spiritual wickedness in high places." (Ephesians 6:11–12)***

You and I are no match for Satan. The Lord told one of his beloved disciples, Peter, that Satan desires to sift him like wheat. But he also says for the human race, "ye are of your father the devil… for he was a liar from the beginning. Listen to what God says in John 8:*44 "ye are of your father the devil, and the lusts of your father ye will do. He was a murderer from the beginning, and abode not in the truth, because there is no truth in him. When he speatheth a lie, he speaketh of his own: for he is a liar, and the father of it."* You may have had no idea that your father was the devil, as many do not, because we live life with blinders on. We are walking (living) by sight and not by faith.

Let's look at how we walk (live) by sight. To understand this, we must understand our makeup. We will discuss this in greater detail later in this book. We are told in the scriptures, and it is true, because we can validate this once we think it through. We are composed of body, soul, and spirit. The body is flesh, bone, and blood; the soul, which is invisible inside of the body, is the controlling entity of the body. In the soul resides the mind, emotion, and will. The body carries out the wishes of the soul. The body makes no decisions. It is only a vessel that carries around the invisible parts of us, which are the soul and spirit. The spirit is that part of us that causes us to worship either the "true God," a god of our making, or the god of this world. God says that you cannot serve two masters. You either hate one and love the other or love the one and hate the other.

In the scriptures, God also calls the soul "flesh" or "self." God talks about the flesh/self in Romans 8:5–9:

> **"For they that are after the flesh do mind the things of the flesh; but they that are after the spirit the things of the spirit. For to be carnally minded [worldly] is death; but to be spiritually minded is life and peace. Because the carnal mind is enmity [deep hatred] against God; for it is not subject to the law of God, neither indeed can be. So then they that are in the flesh cannot please God. But ye [speaking of redeemed believers] are not in the flesh, but in the Spirit, if so that the Spirit of God dwell in you, now if any man have**

not the Spirit of Christ, 'he is none of his.'"

Now let's start with the problems that the body presents—that flesh and blood part of us. Were you aware that the power of sin is in your body? In Romans 7: 18-23, Paul, the author of Romans, says, *"For I know that in me [that is in my flesh] dwelleth no good thing: for to will is present with me, but how to perform that which is good I find not. For the good that I would, I do not; but the evil which I would not, that I do. Now if I do that I would not, it is not I that do it, but sin that dwelleth in me. For I delight in the law of God after the inward man. But I see another law in my members, warring against the law of my mind, and bringing me into captivity to the law of sin which is in my members."*

Members of the body is medical terminology. These are the parts of our bodies that hang off of us—eyes, nose, ears, mouth, hands, arms, feet, genitals, et cetera. They are all physical. Consider what God has to say about the tongue in James 3:3–10:

> *"Behold, we put bits in the horse's mouth, that they may obey us; and we turn about their whole body. Behold also the ships, which thought to be so great, and are driven of fierce winds, yet are turned about with a very small rudder, wither so even the captain turns it. Even so the tongue is a little member, and boasteth great things. Behold how great a matter a little fire kindleth. And the tongue is a fire, a world of sin: so is the tongue among our members, that it defileth the whole body, and setteth on fire the course of nature, and it is set on fire of hell. For every kind of beasts, and of bird, and of serpents, and of things of the sea, is tamed of man. But the tongue can no man tame; it is an unruly evil, full of deadly poison. Therewith bless we God, even the father; and therewith curse we men, which are made after*

the similitude of God."

Men and women, young and old, place beads and rings in their tongues for devious sexual encounters: men with men and women with women. The tongue and nose are used for drug sniffing and tasting. Alcoholics use their tongues for alcohol tasting and drinking. Government officials use their tongues for making false promises to get elected to office. Once there, they forget about the agendas they proclaimed and do things to enable themselves to stay in office. The president of the United States has lied for nearly four years to the people who put their faith in him and now the pandemic has killed a multitude of citizens. Pastors and preachers of many churches have preached for expediency and financial gain instead of preaching the gospel that could save many in their congregations from the wrath and final judgment to come.

Another example of sin in the flesh in using our mouths. With our mouth we may get a single scoop of ice cream. We get one scoop today and tomorrow we get two scoops, and before long we are expecting several scoops. But we started out with one, which was enough. You can take any food item and notice how it turns into gluttony. Same with alcohol or drugs; it starts out as a small drink or a little drug use (perhaps even as a kid), and before long we are hooked (the power of sin). Gluttony is a sin in God's eyes.

Consider tattoos on the body. A person gets one and then another and before long they are all over their body. Things we love to hear and watch are very degrading, such as music and comedy shows, rap music that incites crime (power of sin in flesh), and sexual sin, which is very destructive to the body. A person has sex and enjoys it as a teenager and continues having it into adulthood outside of marriage. Men began having sex with men and women began having sex with women. This is a sin in the body that God hates. In fact, he destroyed the whole city of Sodom and Gomorrah because of sexual sins. Listen to what God says in 1 Corinthians 6:9. *"Know ye not that the unrighteous shall not inherit the kingdom of God? Be not deceived: neither fornicators, nor idolators; nor adulterers, nor effeminate nor abusers of themselves with mankind. Nor thieves, nor covetous, nor drunkards, nor revilers, nor extortioners, shall inherit the Kingdom of God."*

Folks, listen: there is power of sin in your body that you and I cannot overcome. There is a solution, but not within us!

Let's talk a little about the soul, which houses the emotions, mind, and will. The soul is also called "flesh" in the scriptures. We will talk about that later in the book. But listen to what God says about the soul in Ezekiel 18:4. *"Behold, all souls are mine; the soul of the father, so also the soul of the son is mine: the soul that sinneth, it shall die."* Now consider further in James 1:13:

> **"Let no man say when he is tempted, I am tempted of God: for God cannot be tempted with evil, neither tempted he any man. But every man is tempted when he is drawn away of his own mind and enticed. Then when lust hath conceived, it bringeth forth sin; and when sin is finished, it bringeth forth death."**

People do what makes sense to them, and it all starts in the mind. What our physical senses are exposed to determines how we think. Consider what God says in 2 Corinthians 3:3–4. "But if our gospel [good news] be hid, it is hid to them that are lost; in which the god of this world [Satan] hath blinded the minds of them which believe not." The worldly expression is true—"the mind is a terrible thing to waste." Then why waste it?

Here are a few examples of wasted minds. We often hear of about "think tanks" resolving problems of the world. We are impressed with minds of scientific explorers who devise rockets to go into outer space, to the moon or Mars, et cetera. God created the heavens and the earth, and placed man where He wanted man—on earth. The book of Ecclesiastes speaks of vanity. Nothing that we do has not been tried before. In Genesis, man attempted to build the tower of Babel to heaven and God confounded their languages so they couldn't understand one another. When they were asked for bricks, they sent up mortar, et cetera. Therefore, man had to separate from each other; each followed the ones that spoke his language. Space exploration is just another attempt of man disguising his true intent—to go to heaven where God resides.

We have lower courts and high courts to judge one another. Consider Romans 2:4–3: "Therefore thou are inexcusable, O man, whosoever them that judgest; for wherein thou judge another, thou condemnest thyself; for thou that judgest doest the same things. But we are sure that the judgement of God is according to truth against them which commit such things. And thinkest thou this, O man, that judgest them which do such things, and doest the same, that thou shalt escape the judgement of God."

Doctors and scientists dabbling in creation, trying to create test tube babies or trying to alter genes to create what they call superior human beings. Minds can be deceived. The Lord God said there are three enemies of man: attractiveness of the world; the flesh; and the devil. These all create deceptions of the mind. The Lord Jesus has promised that He will return to this world one day. Nevertheless, man has already been prepared for deception by Satan to distort the return of Christ to the earth. Mankind has toyed with the idea of the existence of UFOs to explain away the return of Christ. Consider what the scripture says about Christ's return. After Christ had been crucified, buried, and had risen from the dead, this is the conversation He had with His disciples in Acts 1:6–11:

"When they (disciples) therefore were come together, they asked of him saying, Lord, wilt thou at this time restore again the Kingdom to Israel? And he said unto them, it is not for you to know the times or the seasons which the Father hath put in his own power. But you shall receive power, after that the Holy Ghost is come upon you, and ye shall be witnesses unto Me both in Jerusalem, and in all Judea, and in Samaria, and unto the uttermost part of the earth. When he had spoken these things, while they beheld, he was taken up; and a cloud received him out of their sight. And while they looked steadfastly toward heaven as he went up, behold two men stood by them in white apparel… which also said, ye men of Galilee, why stand ye gazing up into heaven? This same Jesus, which is taken up from you into heaven, shall so come in like manner as ye have seen him go into heaven."

Now let's turn to 1 Thessalonians 4:13–18. Paul was talking to a group of believers and this is what he said:

"But I would not have you to be ignorant, brethren, concerning them which are asleep, that ye sorrow not, even as others which have no hope. For if we believe that Christ

died and rose again, even so then those also which sleep in Jesus will Christ bring with him, for this we say unto you by the word of the Lord, that we which are alive and remain unto the calling of the Lord shall not prevent [proceed] them which are asleep. For the Lord himself shall descent from heaven with a shout, with the voice of the archangel and with the trump of God: and the dead in Christ shall rise first. Then we which are alive and remain shall be caught up together with them in the clouds to meet the Lord in the air: and so shall we ever be with the Lord. Therefore comfort one another with these words."

"Living life with blinders on" will not allow you to receive this truth. Unsaved men and Satan will say some aliens from UFOs have kidnapped millions of people when really their disappearance will have happened through what God calls the "rapture."

There is another cultural aspect of the mind that appears harmless and commendable. There are a lot of churchgoers whose lives are slightly different from other churchgoers, but which in reality are the same. They attend Sunday school or Bible education school, sing in the choirs, volunteer as greeters, ushers, deacons, or even preachers at the pulpit. Listen to what God says in scripture. Consider Matthew 7:21: *"Not everyone that saith unto me, Lord, Lord, shall enter into the kingdom of heaven; but he that doest the will of my father which is in heaven. Many will say to me in that day, Lord, Lord have we not prophesized in thy name? And in thy name have cast out devils, and in thy name done many wonderful works?"* Matthew 7:23 says, *"And then will I profess unto them, I never knew you; depart from me, ye that work iniquity." Another example of "living life with blinders on."* Again, the Lord Jesus said that there are wheat and tares in the church (meaning saved and unsaved people) but not to put them out because in trying to remove the tares (the unsaved), you may uproot the wheat. This, He said, will be done by the angels.

Many people spend a lot of their life being public servants, working in (good) charitable organizations, organizing groups to protest injustices, developing organizations to fight for human rights, equality (racial equality, sexual equality, etc.), and advocating for the homeless, the poor, and the disadvantaged. All of these causes are noble and just but are really just manifestations of the mind to make one feel good.

There are others who love the adoration and recognition given to them by society, such as sports figures, hall of fame inductees, movie stars who win Academy Awards, singers and musicians, politicians who may receive awards for merit, those who earn academic, scientific, legal or medical achievements, those who have streets or buildings named after them, and the list goes on. But the Lord Jesus says you have your reward already. He also asks what profit a man gets in gaining the whole world and lose his own soul.

Listen to what God says in Exodus 20:5. *"Thou shalt not bow thyself to them (things that you praise so highly; you have made them god's pursuits) nor serve them; for I the Lord thy God am a jealous God, visiting the iniquity of the fathers upon the children unto the third and fourth generation of them that hate me."*

Serving oneself is hating God. Consider what God says in Romans 8:5–8: *"For they that are after the flesh [soul] do mind the things of the flesh… for to be carnally minded is death… Because the carnal mind is enmity against God; for it is not subject to the law of God, neither indeed can be…so then they that are in the flesh cannot please God."*

Truly the mind of man will be the eternal downfall of man. The will of man is controlled by the mind of man. How can we prove this? Consider this example. Suppose someone told a group of people that water was good to drink; then another person told the same group of people that gasoline was good to drink, and different people believed both and some drank water and some drank gasoline. Now the question. Which ones would die—the ones that drank water or the ones that drank gasoline? Satan and God are after the same element of man—the mind and will. Whoever gets the mind of man also gets his will. The will determines what you do. The mind gathers information, and the will carry out what the mind has believed is true.

The information given to the mind (correct or incorrect) determines the action that a person takes. This is why the Lord tells us in 2 Corinthians 13:5 to *"Examine yourselves, whether ye be in the faith, prove your own selves. Know ye not your own selves, know that Jesus Christ is in you, except ye be reprobates?"*

The spirit of man is that part of man that allows him to worship. The Lord Jesus told the Samaritan woman (the woman at the well) that she worshipped who she knew not… for God is a spirit and those that worship Him must worship Him in spirit and in truth. We will expound on this later in the book.

But listen to what God says to a group of people in Colossians 2:18–23.

"Let no man beguile you of your reward in a voluntary humility and worshipping of angels, intruding into those things which he hath not seen, vainly puffed up by his

fleshly mind. And not holding the head, from which all of the body by joints and bands having nourishment ministered, and knit together, increased with the increase of God.

Wherefore if ye be dead with Christ from the rudiments of the world, why, as though living in the world, are ye subject to ordinances. Touch not; taste not; handle not. Which all we to perish with the using; after the commandments and doctrine of men?

Which things have indeed a show of wisdom in will – worship and humility and neglecting of the body; not in any honor to the satisfying of the flesh."

There are religious organizations and faiths that are not of God. Take for instance a very large organization that has rituals of confession to a priest. Listen to what God says in 1 Timothy 2:5. *"For there is one God and one mediator between God and men, the man Christ Jesus."* Listen to what God says to those whose blinders have been removed from their eyes in 1 John 1:8–9. *"If we say we have no sin, we deceive ourselves, and the truth is not in us. If we confess our sins, he is faithful and just to forgive us our sins, and to cleanse us from all unrighteousness."*

These priests set themselves up for a fall. They declare themselves as having special gifts. One such gift is the gift of being a eunuch. Unfortunately, because many of them do not have this gift, they end up molesting young boys. Listen to what God says

1 Corinthians 6:18. *"Flee fornication. Every sin that a man doeth is without the*

body; but he that committeth fornication sinneth against his own body."

Another admonition is from Paul in 1 Corinthians 7:7. *"For I would that all men were even as I myself. But every man hath his proper gift of God, one after this, and another after that. I say therefore to the married and widows. It is great for them if they abide even as I am." 1 Corinthians 7:9 says, "But if they cannot contain, let them marry; for it is better to marry than to burn."*

There are other religious groups that hand out magazines and pamphlets. They want to share with you what "their" bible says but not the Holy Bible of God. Listen to what God says about this group in 2 John verses: 7-11:

> *"For many deceivers are entered into the world, who confess not that Jesus Christ is come in the flesh. This is a deceiver and an antichrist. Look to yourselves, that we lose not those things which we have wrought, but that we receive a full reward. Whosoever transgresseth and abideth not in the doctrine in Christ, hath not God. He that abideth in the doctrine of Christ, he hath both the Father and the Son. If there come any unto you and bring not this doctrine, receive him not into your house, neither bid him Godspeed. For he that biddeth him Godspeed is partaker of his evil deeds."*

Some pretty strong words, don't you think? There are other church groups that have women as their pastors. Listen to what God says about this matter starting in Ephesians 4:7. *"But unto every one of us is given grace according to the measure of the gift of Christ." Verse 10 says, "He that descended is the same also that ascended up far above all heavens, that he might fill all things. And he gave some, apostles, and some prophets, and some evangelists; and some pastors and teachers. For the perfecting of the saints, for the work of the ministry, for the edifying of the body of Christ. These are gifts that Christ gave. Other gifts were and are given by the Holy Spirit."*

Then Christ gives the qualifications of a pastor/bishop in 1 Timothy 3:1–2. *"This is a true saying, If a man desire the office of a bishop, he desireth a good work…a bishop/pastor then must be blameless, the "husband of one wife." A female cannot fit this description and qualifications. Unfortunately, Satan is able to enter into all religions and faiths. Even the ones that are closer to correct, Satan has entered into and created an environment that has turned a relationship with Christ into a religion. Satan has even counterfeited "salvation" in many churches. Another example of "living life with blinders on."*

God created man to worship Him, but that was destroyed from the beginning by Adam's first son, Cain. God in Genesis 4:1–9 says, *"And Adam knew Eve his wife and she conceived, and bore Cain, and said, I have gotten a man from the Lord, then she again bore his brother Abel. And Abel was a keeper of the sheep, but Cain was a tiller of the ground. And in the process of time it came to pass, that Cain brought of the fruit of the ground as an offering unto the Lord… And Abel, he also brought of his firstling of his flock and of the fat thereof. And the Lord had respect unto Abel and to his offering. But unto Cain and to his offering he had no respect. And Cain was very wroth, and his countenance fell."*

Pause. Obviously, God had given instruction to Adam how He preferred to be worshipped. Remember earlier in the garden when Adam had disobeyed God, he and his wife, Eve, hid themselves in the garden and covered themselves with fig leaves to cover their nakedness. When God came to the garden and asked them why were they hiding, they said because they were naked and God asked them, "Who told you that you were naked?" So God killed an animal to get the skin to cover their nakedness. This was the first principle that God required: the blood of an innocent animal as a payment for sin. In fact, he tells us in Hebrews 9:22, *"All things are by the Law [God's law] cleansed with blood and without the shedding of blood is no forgiveness of sin."*

This information obviously was told to Cain and Abel by their father, Adam. But Cain decided how he wanted to worship God. There are a lot of Cains today who have decided how they are going to worship God. Listen to Christ as He speaks to the Samaritan woman at the well in John 4:19–24:

> ***"The woman saith unto him, Sir, I perceive that thou art a prophet. Our father worshiped in this mountain; and ye say that in Jerusalem is the place where men ought to worship. Jesus saith unto her, woman, believe me, the hour cometh, when ye shall neither in this mountain, nor yet at Jerusalem, worship the Father. Ye worship ye know not what: we know what we worship. For salvation is of the Jews. But the hour cometh, and now is, when the true worshippers shall worship the Father in spirit and in truth; For the Father seeketh such to worship him. God is a Spirit and they that worship him must worship him in spirit and in truth."***

Later in the scriptures, Christ says that He is the truth and the light; no one gets to the Father except by Him. Man cannot worship God anyway he wants. But to this very day, man thinks that going to a church building is the proper way to worship God. For God also says that He no longer dwells in buildings made by hands. Basically, what He was telling the woman at the well is that you must have the spirit of God in you to worship God, who is spirit. Spirit to spirit is the only way you can worship God. In other words, you must be a child of God in order to worship Him. In Romans 8:8–9 God says,

"They that are in the flesh cannot please God. But ye are not in the flesh [speaking of believers] but in the Spirit; if so be that the Spirit of God dwell in you. Now if any man have not the Spirit of Christ, he is none of his."

Thinking that you can worship and please God without the Spirit of God in you is still another example of "living life with blinders on."

It is imperative that we stop in the "business of life" and begin to ask the right questions concerning our existence. You owe it to yourself, while you yet live, while blood is flowing warm in your body. What is beyond the grave? Please do not continue to live in this life with blinders on. It doesn't matter what race or sex you are; you must remember God has no respect of persons… rich or poor, well-educated or not well-educated, everyone has the same opportunity and the same amount of time. There are sixty seconds in a minute, sixty minutes in an hour, twenty-four hours in a day, 365 days in a year, ten years in a decade, et cetera. We all have the same amount of time. If you value life, then you must value time, because that's what life is made of.

When God created the world, He said it was good. When God created man (Adam), He said that was good. He gave man (Adam) dominion over everything He created, and He said to everything "be fruitful and multiply." He said He placed a seed in everything to reproduce after its own kind; therefore, Adam had within his genes the seed to reproduce after his kind; his first fruit (son, child) was Cain, and then Abel, and so on. Because man (Adam) disobeyed God, he was cursed. Therefore, the entire human race inherited that curse; for the entire human race was in the genes of Adam. But the fallen angel (Satan) had a lot to do with what happened to man, for he deceived the woman, who in turn convinced the man Adam to disobey God.

As a result of this act, man has disobeyed God ever since. Man has come to disrespect God and, in so doing, disrespected man. When God created men and women, He created them to be equal, but some have come to believe that some men and women are superior to others because of race or inheritance, not recognizing that we all have been cursed and that you are only demonstrating the fact of this curse.

Pause. Let's ponder the followings questions in the following chapters of this book:

Question I: Who are we?

Question II: What must we know?

Question III: What is expected of us?

Question IV: Where do we get this information?

To not get answers to these questions will cause us to live life here on earth "with blinders on." For God says in Hebrews 9:27, *"For it is appointed unto men once to die and after that the judgement."* Listen also to God in John 3:17: *"For God sent not his Son unto the world to condemn the world."* He added to the discussion on condemnation by saying, in verse 18, *"He that believeth on him is not condemned, but he that believeth not is condemned already."* If no one had taken the time to share this with you, you would not have known that you were born headed to hell.

In Romans 5:12 it states: *"Wherefore, as by one man (Adam) sin entered into the world, and death by sin; so death passed upon all men, for that all have sinned."* And verse 19 states, *"For as by one man's disobedience man were made sinners."*

Question: How does one get to God? The Lord Jesus said no one gets to the Father unless the Father draws them to Him.

He said there is none that seeketh after Him.

Question: How is this done?

Let's go to the Word of God again. Christ was talking to His disciples when He said this in John 16:7–11. *"Nevertheless I tell you the truth; it is expedient for you that I go away; for if I not go away [by death back to heaven] the Comforter [the third person of the God Head… the Holy Spirit] will not come unto you; but if I depart, I will send him unto you. And when he is come, he will convict the world of sin, and of righteousness, and of judgement. Of sin, because they [man] believe not on me; of righteousness, because "I" go to my father, and ye see me no more."*

Listen carefully… "of righteousness because I go to my father." The righteousness of God is not an act, behavior, or any other thing. The righteousness of God is a person, and that person is the Lord Jesus Christ. There is absolutely nothing you or I could do to make us right with God, so stop trying! Just accept what God says.

Let's continue with verse 11. *"Of judgement, because the Prince of this world [Satan] has been judged already."* Satan's goal is to help keep blinders on your eyes until you die so he will have company in the lake of fire where he and all unsaved persons will burn forever and ever.

Let's talk about the historical coming of the Holy Spirit. Look at Acts 2:2-6 *"And when the day of Pentecost was fully come, all of the disciples [120 of them] were all in one accord in one place. And suddenly there came a sound from heaven as of a rushing mighty wind; and it filled all in the house where they were sitting. And there appeared upon them cloven tongues like as of fire, and it sat upon each of them. And they were all filled with the holy God [God's spirit], and began to speak with other tongues [other languages, not known by them] as the Spirit gave them utterance. And those that were dwelling at Jerusalem Jews, devout men, out of every nation under heaven. Now when this was noised abroad, the multitude came together, and were confounded, because that every man heard them speak in his own language."*

This was the coming of the Holy Spirit that Christ had promised, before he went to the cross to be crucified and ascended back to Heaven. So now we (you and I) live in the dispensation of the Holy Spirit to this very day. Remember his role was and is (1) to convict men of sin, (2) of judgment, and (3) of righteousness.

Pause. The Lord Jesus said no one comes to the father (God) unless He draws them to Him. And how is that done? He (His Holy Spirit) convicts (makes one feel guilty of the things he does/ has done, or should have done) us of sin. When you read the four Gospels (Matthew, Mark, Luke, and John) of the New Testament, you will often hear Christ say, "He that has ears to hear, let him hear," following many statements He made. Not all will hear, for many reasons and excuses. Many because they don't want to change. Listen, not all sins seem terribly bad, but like Baskin Robbins having many different flavors of ice cream, it's still ice cream, so there are different kinds of sin, but they are all still sin!

It doesn't matter who you are or what you have or have not done— you are still a sinner.

And the wages of sin (what you earn) is death (the lake of fire), the second death.

Remember, every man will experience the first death (which is of the body). Don't forget the curse given to Adam back in Genesis. Remember, Adam is the head of the first human race and "all in Adam must die." All in Adam have been condemned already. Therefore, unless you get out of the family of Adam and into Christ who is the last Adam and the head of the "second human race," the lake of fire is your eternal abode.

So how is this done? You must be "born again." That new birth is a spiritual birth that comes from above (Heaven). It's a gift for everyone who "has ears to hear what the scripture tells us." It's what God calls *grace*. Grace is unmerited favor from God for everyone who believes it.

Listen to what Christ said in Matthew 13:15. *"For these people's heart is waxed gross, and their ears are dull of hearing, and their eyes they have closed, lest at any time they should see with their eyes and hear with their ears and should understand with their heart, and should be converted [born again]."*

Some will say, "But he has a good heart; he means well." Do you want God to judge you on the basis of your heart? I don't think so. Listen to what He says about your heart in Proverbs 23:7. *"For as he thinketh in his heart, so is he."* Now what do you think with? Yes, you think with your mind, and that's what God has reference to when he talks about your heart. Listen again in Jeremiah 17:9: *"The heart is deceitful above all things, and desperately wicked; who can know it."* So, a person is in trouble if he wants to be judged by his heart!

Pause and listen carefully. 1 John 2:15–17 says, *"God says Love not the world, neither the things that are of the world. If my man loves the world, the Love of God is not in him. For all that is in the world, the love of flesh, and the lust of the eyes, and the pride of life, is not of God, but is of the world. And the world will pass away, and the rest thereof: but he that doeth the will of God abideth forever."* He continues in Galatians 5:19: "Now the works of the flesh [soul and body] are manifest," which are these: Adultery, fornication, sexual impurity, sexual excess, idolatry (putting one's chief affections on any object or person instead of God), witchcraft (sorcery) tampering with the powers of evil, dabbling in the occult, variance (strife and discord), emulations (jealousy, selfambition, dissensions, heresies (permanent organized divisions), envying, murders, drunkenness, revellings (excess eating or gluttony), carousing and the like. I tell you now as I have told you before that they which do such things shall not inherit the kingdom of God.

One of man's chief problems in this country is that he does not accept the righteousness of God. Instead, we go about establishing our own set of rules to live by, such as our constitution, bylaws, federal laws, state laws and local laws, and we ignore the laws of God written in each person's heart (conscience). We determine what is right and what is wrong. What a travesty, when we were born law breakers, disobedient and sinful. We are sinners, and just as fruit trees produce fruit, sinners produce sin.

Pause. There is hope. The good news is that God has already developed a plan to save us if we only take the time to listen, understand, and obey! This plan was established before the creation of the world, along with Adam and Eve. God knew from the beginning that Adam was going to disobey, but because of God's love He gave Adam and Eve a free will, to love Him and obey or not love Him and disobey. We inherited that same will to obey and live or disobey and die (eternal death). The only way we can learn of God's plan is totally from His written Word—the Bible.

Listen to this in Hebrews 9:22. *"Almost all things are by the law purged [cleansed] with blood, and without shedding of blood is no remission [forgiveness of sin]."* Let's go back to the beginning in Genesis when Adam and Eve first disobeyed God. In Genesis 3:4, it says, *"And the serpent said to Eve, ye shall not surly die for God doth know that in the day ye eat thereof, then your eyes shall be opened, and ye shall be as gods, knowing good and evil."* After they both ate the fruit, the eyes of both of them were opened, they knew that they were naked.

Folks, this is what sin does for us. It exposes our nakedness. So, Adam and Eve sewed fig leaves together and made themselves aprons. Genesis 3:8 says, *"And they heard the voice of the Lord God walking in the garden in the cool of the day and Adam and Eve hid themselves from the presence of God amongst the trees. And the Lord God called unto Adam and said where art thou and he said I heard thy voice in the garden and I was afraid, because I was naked and I hid myself."*

Pause. Listen to a truth in Hebrews 4:13. *"Neither is there any creature that is not manifested in his sight: but all things are naked and opened unto the eyes of him with whom we have to do."*

Now back to the garden and Genesis 5:11. *"And the Lord God said, who told thee that thou wast naked? Hast thou eaten of the tree, where of I commanded thee that thou shouldest not eat?"* And 5:21: *"Unto Adam also and to Eve the Lord God made them coats of skin and clothed them."*

In order for God to give them coats of skin, He had to shed the blood of an animal. This is the first message of blood for sin. Don't forget this. It's very important, for God tells us in Leviticus 17:14,

"The life of the flesh is in the blood." Your doctors can tell you a lot about your ailments when they order your blood work. When the blood turns cold in your vessels, you are dead from whatever the cause—accidents, murder, heart attack, et cetera. The life of the flesh is in the blood.

Let's continue with the blood issue. In Exodus 12, the Lord was speaking to Moses and Aaron, when He was initiating the "Passover." The Israelites were being released out of slavery from Egypt. Verse 5 says, *"Your lamb shall be without blemish, a male of the first year; ye shall take it from the sheep or from the goat and ye shall keep it up until the fourteenth day of the same month; and the whole assembly of the congregation of Israel shall kill it in the evening."*

Verse 7 says, *"And they shall take of the blood, and strike it on the two side posts and on the upper door post of the houses, wherein they shall eat it."*

Continue to read down to verse 13: *"And the blood shall be for a token upon the houses where ye are: and when "I" see the blood, I will "pass over" you, and the plague shall not be upon you to destroy you, while I smite the hand of Egypt."* Now let me ask you one simple question. God said when He sees the blood, He will pass over them. Who is the blood for? The blood is for God!

Throughout the Old Testament, God required a blood sacrifice for the sins of the people after the Israelites left Egypt. It was performed by priests whom God had chosen to perform these duties.

We read the following in Matthew 1:18, the first book of the New Testament:

"Now the birth of Jesus Christ was on this wise: when as his mother Mary was espoused to Joseph before they came together, she was found with child of the Holy Ghost. Then Joseph her husband, being a just man, and not willing to make her a public example, was minded to put her away privately. But while he thought on these things, behold the angel of the Lord appeared to him in a dream, saying Joseph, thy son of David, fear not to take unto thee Mary thy wife, for that which is conceived in her is of the Holy Ghost. And she shall bring forth a son, and thou shalt call him Jesus: for he shall save his people from their sins."

Now all this was done so that it might be fulfilled which was spoken of the Lord by the prophets, in verse 23: *"Behold, a virgin shall be with child, and shall bring a son, and then shall call His name Immanuel," which is interpreted as "God with us."*

Let's recall what is said back in Genesis verses 14–15: *"And the Lord said unto the serpent... And I will put enmity between thee and the woman, and between thy seed and her seed; [speaking of Christ born of a woman by the Holy Ghost] it shall bruise thy head [a killing blow for the human race], and thou shalt bruise his heel."* Which is the most telling blow, one to the heel or one to the head?

Pause. Remember, Christ could not come by the seed of Adam. Adam was sinful but Christ was sinless. Listen to Romans 5:12. *"Wherefore, as by one man [Adam] sin entered into the world, and death by sin: and so death passed upon all men, for that all have sinned."*

Romans 5:18 states, *"Therefore by the offense of one, judgement came upon all men unto condemnation; even so by the righteousness of one the free gift came upon all men unto justification of life. For as by one man's disobedience many were made sinners, so by the obedience of one shall many be made righteous."*

Pause. Listen to 1 Timothy 3:15. *"And without controversy great is the mystery of godliness. God was manifest in the flesh, justified in the spirit, seen of angels, preached unto the Gentiles, believed on in the world, received up into glory."*

Another great observation found in the early chapter of all the gospel writers, Matthew, Mark, Luke, and John. Let's take Matthew. As John the Baptist was preaching and baptizing, Matthew 3:11 states, *"He said I indeed baptize you with water unto repentance; but he that cometh after me is mightier than I, whose shoes I am not worthy to bear: he shall baptize you with the Holy Ghost, and with fire."*

In another gospel, John the Baptist looked around and saw Christ coming to be baptized by him, and said, "Behold the Lamb of God who cometh to take away the sins of the world." In Matthew 4:15 it states, *"And Jesus, when he was baptized, went up straightway out of the water." Verse 10 states, "The heavens were opened unto him, and he saw the Spirit of God descending like a dove, and lighting upon him. And lo a voice from heaven, saying this is my beloved son, in whom I am well pleased."*

Question: Who is Jesus?

That's a very good question. Let's let the scriptures tell us.

John 1:1 states, *"In the beginning was the word, and the word was with God, and the word was God. The same was in the beginning with God. All things were made by him, and without him was not anything made that was made. In him was life; and the life was the light of men."* Verse 10 states, *"He was in the world, and the world was made by him, and the world knew him not. He came unto his own [Jesus] and his own received him not. But as many as received him, to them, he gave power to become the sons of God, even to them that believed on his name. Which were born, not of blood, nor of the will of the flesh, nor of the will of man, but of God." Verse 14 states, "And the word was made flesh, and dwelt among us [and we beheld his glory, the glory as of the only begotten of the father] full of Grace and truth." Listen carefully.* The word was God and the word was made flesh, who we know as the Lord Jesus Christ.

Listen again. In 1 John 5:20, it states, *"And we know that the son of God is come, and hath given us an understanding that we may know him that is true, and we are in him that is true, even in his son Jesus Christ. This is the true God, and eternal life."*

The Lord Jesus said that he was the way, the truth and the life, no one gets to the Father except by Him. In 1 Timothy 2:5, God states, "For there is one God, and one mediator between God and men, the man Christ Jesus."

Pause. Why is Jesus so important for you and me to obtain eternal life? To have our names placed unto the book of life, to become members of the Lord's human race where Christ is the head, to become children of God, to become members of God's family, and to live forever with Him?

Remember, that blood principle started in the garden. In Exodus, God gave the Israelites instructions to paint blood over the door posts for deliverance. God told Abraham that through him all of the nations of the world would be blessed. Remember, Christ came in the line of Abraham.

Listen again in Luke 9:22, where it states, *"The son of man must suffer many things, and be rejected of the elders and chief priests and scribes, and be slain and be raised the third day."*

In John 7:32, *the Pharisees and the people murmured such things concerning Jesus; and the Pharisees and the chief priests sent officers to take him. Then Jesus said unto them, "Yet a little while I am with you, and then I go unto him that sent me. Ye shall seek me, and shalt not find me; and where I am thither ye cannot come." Continue to verse 37: "In the last day, that great day of the feast, Jesus stood and cried, saying, 'If any man thirst, let him come unto to me and drink He that believeth in me, as the scripture hath said, out of his belly shall flow rivers of living water."*

Verse 39 states, *"But this spake he of the spirit, which they that believe on him should receive," for the Holy Ghost was not yet given; because Jesus was not yet glorified.*

Remember, man was cursed body, soul, and spirit, and Christ was speaking of man receiving the spirit of God for all that believed the record.

Now, listen to what God has to say about the record (the Bible) in 1 John 5:7. *"For there are three that bear record in heaven, the Father, the Son, and the Holy Ghost: and these three are one. And there are three that bear witness in earth, the spirit, and the water, and the blood, these three agree in one."*

If we receive the witness of men—yes, we do—when you go grocery shopping and you purchase a can of beans or tomatoes or any other food, we don't question whether there are beans or tomatoes in that can… do we? No, we don't. Why not trust God? He is greater and He cannot lie.

John 5:9 states, *"If we receive the witness of men, the witness of God is greater: for this is the witness of God which he has testified of his son. He that believeth in the son of God hath the witness in himself; he that believeth not God hath made him a liar, because he believeth not the record that God gave of his Son."*

What do you believe? Let's talk about beliefs. Some believe that if they are good, they will be saved. Intelligent people with good hearts who feed the poor, help the little people who can't help themselves, feel pity for the homeless, feel sorry for the mistreated and racially discriminated upon, are against racism of any kind, attend church, confess to the priest (Catholics), do meditation, pray every day in groups, wear special clothing to cover their bodies, act very pious, do fasting, and the list goes on. But did you hear what God said? "He that believeth in the son hath eternal life."

What is it that man must believe about the son of God, the Lord Jesus, the second person of the God head? What does it mean to believe? To believe is to have faith, trust, reliance, to be fully convinced.

Let's look at an example I heard some time ago. There was a Bible translator visiting a country where he couldn't speak the language. So he sat in a chair and lifted his feet off the ground and asked the translator to give him a word that described what he was doing. The translator gave him a word that meant "putting your whole weight upon." Well, that's what it means to believe.

Faith is belief in action. Whatever you believe, it is followed by action; otherwise, it's just vain rhetoric… worthless. What then must you believe? Hebrews 2:9 states, *"But we see Jesus, who was made a little lower than the angels for the suffering of death, crowned with glory and honor; that by the grace of God should taste death for every man."* When did this happen? Over two thousand years ago. It took place at the crucifixion of an innocent man, Jesus, who knew no sin.

Listen to what John has written in 19:16–30: *"Then delivered him therefore unto them to be crucified and they took Jesus away. And he bearing his cross went forth into a place called the place of a skull,"* which is called in the Hebrew Golgotha. Verse 29 states, *"Now there was set a vessel full of vinegar; and they filled a sponge with vinegar, and put it into his mouth."*

Verse 30 states, *"When Jesus therefore had received the vinegar, he said, 'It is finished' and he bowed his head and gave up the ghost"* (His spirit; remember, body, soul, and spirit). Listen to verse 37: *"But when they came to Jesus, and saw that he was dead already, they brake not his legs: But one of the soldiers with a spear pierced his side, and forthwith came there out blood and water."*

Have you ever seen blood and water come out of a person when they are punctured? What does this mean with Jesus? Remember, when God sees the blood, it satisfied him as a proper sacrifice for the sins of the people. Since Christ is eternal, and so is His sacrifice. But what about the water? God tells us in Ephesians 5:26, *"That he might sanctify and cleanse us with the washing of water by the word."*

Remember, our thoughts are not His thoughts, neither His ways are our ways, and as far as the heavens are above the earth, so are our ways different from His ways and our thoughts different from His. You must forget about how you think you are saved or can be saved by what you have heard. If what you have heard is different from what the Bible says, you are yet in your sins, and the wages of sin is death— the second death, at the judgment seat of Christ. All who are not His and whose names are not in the book of life will be cast unto the lake of fire. Revelation 20:14 states, *"Only Christ is the righteousness of God,"* and He is a person. Listen carefully to 1 Corinthians 1:30: *"But of him are ye in Christ Jesus who of God is made unto us wisdom, and righteousness, and sanctification and redemption."*

In Galatian 3 starting at verse 13, listen what God tells us *"Christ hath redeemed us from the curse of the law, being made a curse for us: for it is written, cursed is every one that hangeth on a tree."* This is the GOOD News OF THE GOSPEL. God is very adamite about for he says in Galatians 1: 8-*9* *"But though we, or an angel from heaven, preach any other gospel unto you than that which we have preached unto you, let him be accursed. As we said before, so say I now again, if any man preach any other gospel than that ye have received, let him be accursed!!!!"*

The work of Christ on the cross accomplished the redemption work of Christ. Redemption means that He purchased us back from the god of this world, and He offers this to every man, woman, and child as a free gift to everyone that believes it and places their trust and faith in Christ. Jesus has been made our savior by God. Listen again as God tells us in Acts 2:36. *"Therefore let all the house of Israel know assuredly, that God hath made that same Jesus, whom ye have crucified, both Lord and Christ. Therefore Christ became the propitiation [satisfaction for God]."* Consider 1 John 2:2, which states, *"And he is the propitiation for our sins: and not for our sins only, but also for the sins of the whole world."*

This is the good news that is spoken of by many believers. It's found in 1 Corinthians 15:3–4, when Paul states, *"For I delivered unto you first of all that which I received, how that Christ died for our sins according to the scripture; And he was buried and that he rose again the third day according to the scriptures."*

Listen, folks, you must believe this. It's your only hope. This is given to us as a free gift. We did not earn it, nor did we deserve it. Ephesians 2:8–9 states, *"For by grace are ye saved through faith; and that not of yourselves; it is a gift of God not of works, lest any man should boast."*

Let's take a little peek into the future in speaking of Christ in 1 Corinthians 15:24–26. *"Then cometh the end, when he shall have delivered up the kingdom to God, even the father; when he shall have put down all rule and authority and power. For he must reign, till he hath put all enemies under his feet. The last enemy that shall be destroyed is death."*

Now that you have all this information, what are you going to do with it? If you desire to exercise your desire (belief and faith), the Lord tells us what to do in His Word. His Word is what's important, not what I say or what anyone else says. God tells us in 1 Peter 1:23: *"Being born again, not corruptible seed [man's word] but of incorruptible, by the word [Bible] of God, which liveth and abideth forever."*

This is the promise that God has made to me and you: He tells us in Revelations 3:20, *"Behold, I stand at the door, and knock, if any man hear my voice, and open the door, I will come in to him, and will sup with him, and he with me."*

Now listen very, very closely. In Romans 10:9–10, it states, *"That if thou confess with thy mouth that Jesus is Lord, and shalt believe in thine heart [mind] that God hath raised him from the dead, thou shalt be saved. For with the heart [mind] believeth unto righteousness; and with the mouth confession is made unto salvation."* It's just that simple. Now go ahead and pray this prayer and express yourself to Him. He is listening, for He never sleeps nor slumbers… go ahead!

Let me help you. "Lord God, I know now that I am a sinner and have sinned against You and am worthy of death. I was born a sinner without any hope and I now understand that You sent Your son to die for me on the cross. I believe that He did die and was buried and rose again on the third day. You promised if I accepted Your son's death as payment for my sins that You would give me the free gift of eternal life. I am eternally grateful for Your love and grace. Thank You, Father. Amen."

Now if you truly meant that prayer, you are saved. Your name is now written in the book of life and you have been placed into the body of Christ, which is called the church. The church is not a building that you attend located on the street in many cities. God says He no longer dwells in temples made by hand. Listen to what God says in Acts 7:48. *"Howbeit the most High dwelleth not in temples made with hands; as saith the prophet. Heaven is my throne, and earth is my footstool:*

What house will ye build me? saith the Lord or what is the place of my rest." Remember, God neither sleeps nor slumbers. He's God.

Let's pause for a moment. How does a person know if they are saved? Here again we must believe God, but let's examine your confession. Remember the soul self-houses the mind, will, and emotion (feelings). When we receive salvation, it is like a marriage. In fact, it is a marriage. When you meet someone that you really care for, you may get all excited. That's emotion. And as time passes, you gather more information about this person. That's the function of the mind. Now comes the hard part—the will. After all the excitement and emotions have subsided and you review all of the facts in your mind, now it's decision time. This requires your will. The question is, are you willing to spend the rest of your life with this person? Are you willing to put that person ahead of you in importance? Are you willing to put them first in your life over yourself? If your answer is yes, then you are ready to be married. That is the same procedure you must go through when accepting Christ as your Lord and Savior.

Listen to this order in Ephesians 1:13. *"In whom ye also trusted, after that ye heard the word of truth, the gospel of your salvation: in whom also after that ye believed, ye were sealed with that holy spirit of promise."*

Again, in Matthew 13:15, we read: *"For this people's heart is waxed gross, and their ears are dull of hearing, and their eyes they have closed; Lest at any time they should see with their eyes and hear with their ears, and should understand with their heart [mind] and should be converted and I should heal them."*

Can you see the order? Seeing, hearing, understanding, and acting on what you have heard and understood. All of this requires the work of Holy Spirit. The Holy Spirit uses the Word of God for your emotion (hearing the good news—gospel) so you will understand the blood sacrifice of Christ, who is the only sinless one that's acceptable to God, because He is God. Then you must be willing to act on that information through repentance (forgetting your thoughts as to what pleases God and accepting what God says in the scripture) and by prayer and confession to him.

This is the assurance that God gives us. 1 John 5:10–14 states:

"He that believeth in the Son of God hath the witness in himself: he that believeth not God hath made him a liar; because he believeth not the record that God gave of his son. And this is the record, that God hath given to us eternal life and this life is in his son. He that hath the Son hath Life; and he that hath not the son of God hath not Life…These things have I written unto you that believe on the name of the Son of God; that ye may know that ye have eternal life; and that ye may believe on the name of the Son of God. And this is the confidence that we have in him, that if we ask anything according to his will He hearth us."

We welcome you if you prayed that prayer of repentance and asked Christ to become Lord of your life. In so doing, you became a member of the family of God. Now, your next step is to discover what you have become. In this writing, the goal was to remove the blinders off your eyes. The purpose is not to leave you with partial blinders. We are currently in a viral COVID-19 period, and this could be somewhat of a challenge for you. The next order of business for you is to be water baptized. You need to join a local church fellowship.

This is what the Lord tell us in 1 Peter 3:21. *"The like figure where unto even baptism doth also now save us not putting away of the filth of the flesh, but an answer of a good conscience toward God."*

Another reason to get water baptized is because Christ said that being ashamed to be identified with Him is a strong reason that your prayer of confession may not have been legitimate. Listen to Matthew 10:32-33: *"Whosoever therefore shall confess me before men, him will I confess also before my Father which is in heaven. But whosoever shall deny me before men, him will I also deny before my Father which is in heaven."* You cannot be a silent believer or Christian. Listen further to what God says about any man in Christ. Note this, as it is critical, such that you don't become a believer with "blinders on." 2 Corinthians 5:17–21 states:

"Therefore if any man be in Christ, he is a new creature; old things are passed away; behold all things are become new. And all things are of God, who hath reconciled us to himself by Jesus Christ and hath given to us the ministry of reconciliation. To wit, that God was in Christ reconciling the world unto himself, not imputing their transgressions unto them; but hath

committed unto us the word of reconciliation. Now there we are ambassadors for Christ as though God did beseech you by us, we pray you in Christ's stead, be ye reconciled to God…for he hath made him to be sin for us, who knew no sin; that we might be made the righteousness of God in man."

The goal of this book is to present Christ to you in a prayerful way for you to understand more about your creator God and what He has done to save you and me. God loves us, but it's not His love that saves us…it's His grace. Ephesians 2:8–9 states, *"For by grace are ye saved through faith and not of yourselves; it is a gift of God, not of works, lest any man should boast. Grace is unmerited favor [God having pity on a people who could not help themselves]."* His love would send all of mankind to hell and the lake of fire, which is what we deserve and earned because of who we are and what we have done.

If given the opportunity, I shall write a follow-up book for believers who have "blinders on." Even though they are saved, there are carnal Christians, fleshly Christians, and babes in Christ who need discipling. The Lord Jesus gave us a commandment to all believers. You can find it in all the gospels: Matthew, Mark, Luke, and John. Take Matthew 28:18–20:

"And Jesus came and spoke unto them saying, All power is given unto me in heaven and in earth…Go ye therefore and teach all nations, baptizing them in the name of the Father, and of the Son, and of the Holy Ghost…Teaching them to obey all things whatsoever I have commanded you. And lo, I am with you always, even unto the end of the world."

Amen.

ABOUT THE AUTHOR

Dr. Julius Mosley II was born and raised in St. Petersburg Florida. He graduated from Florida A&M University and attended Howard University Dental School where he obtained his Dental degree. He was a Dental Officer at Travic Air Force Base in California during Vietnam War. He is a practicing dentist for over 40 years, a husband of 37 years to his beautiful wife and a father of three adult children. He is also the ministry head of evangelism and discipleship for over 20 years at his local fellowship, of which he is a member. When he was a fourth-grader, he wanted to find the reason for his existence. He could not accept the fact that he had been created and allowed to live and then not exist anymore. His second desire was to become a dentist so he could help people. He accomplished both. He learned how to receive eternal life and to share this very important information with others while giving God the Glory for all he has done.